From the desktop of Jeffrey Simmons

A vacation in Paris inspired Miroslav Sasek to create childrens travel guides to the big cities of the world. He brought me *This is Paris* in 1958 when I was publishing in London, and we soon followed up with *This is London*. Both books were enormously successful, and his simple vision grew to include more than a dozen books. Their amusing verse, coupled with bright and charming illustrations, made for a series unlike any other, and garnered Sasek (as we always called him) the international and popular acclaim he deserved.

I was thrilled to learn that *This is San Francisco* will once again find its rightful place on bookshelves, and I would like to thank Judith Stonehill and Barbara Cohen of New York Bound Books for their help and enthusiasm in bringing this wonderful gem to the attention of Universe Publishing. Sasek is no longer with us (and I have lost all contact with his family), but I am sure he would be delighted to know that a whole new generation of wide-eyed readers is being introduced to his whimsical, imaginative, and enchanting world.

_____

Your name here

Published by arrangement with Simon & Schuster Books for Young Readers,
Simon & Schuster Children's Publishing Division

This edition first published in 2003 by
UNIVERSE PUBLISHING
A Division of Rizzoli International Publications, Inc.
300 Park Avenue South
New York, NY 10010

2008 2009 2010 2011 2012 / 11 12 13 14 15 16

Printed in China

ISBN-13: 978-0-7893-0962-4

Library of Congress Catalog Control Number: 2003102184

Cover design: centerpointdesign
Universe editor: Jane Ginsberg

M. Sasek

This is
SAN FRANCISCO

UNIVERSE

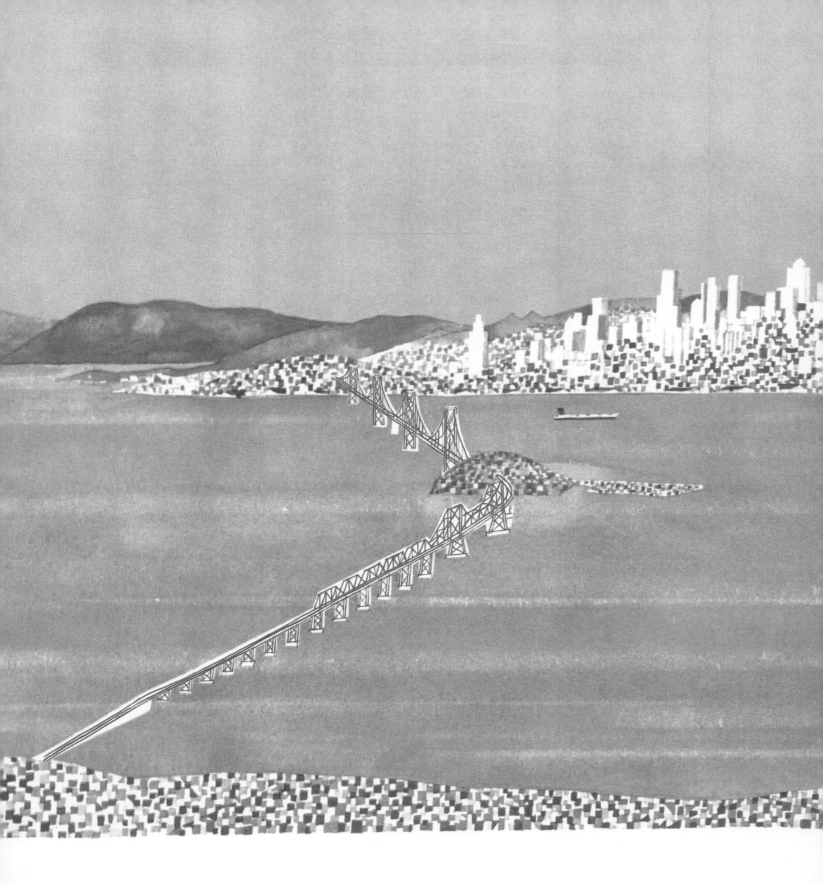

Yerba Buena, a small village established by Spanish colonists from Mexico
186 years ago, came to booming life with the Gold Rush of 1849–51 and with
the discovery of silver in Nevada; in 1906 it was destroyed by earthquake
and fire; rebuilt within three years, it is now one of the most charming, most
cosmopolitan, most beloved cities in the world —

SAN FRANCISCO, city by the Golden Gate, Queen of the West.

"And has only one drawback — 'tis hard to leave."

(Rudyard Kipling)

San Franciscans claim that their city is built on forty-two hills.

You drive down the hill —

Lombard Street — the world's crookedest —

Broadway tunnel —

through the hill —

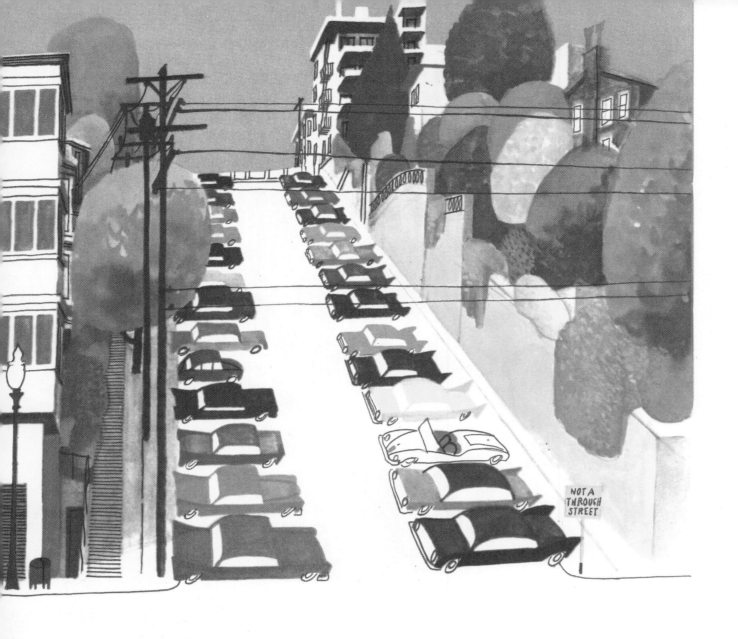

you park on the hill.

Curb your wheels in — or this policeman
will fine you —

and drive carefully — or your car could end on this hill —

— but up hill or down hill — walking is the hardest.

11

Leave the hard work to the cable cars!*

The California Line

The Powell Line

The cable is operated by a gripman:

the grip lever grasps the cable running underground which tows the car.

The first cable car was introduced into the city in 1873.

At the foot of the hill the cable car is turned on the turntable.

The crossing is controlled
by the signalman.

Children are not permitted to hang on the outside.

But once on the hill — the view is your reward:

the sky, the hills, the bridges, the ships and the Bay — one of the
largest, finest and safest landlocked harbors in the world!

Telegraph Hill with Coit Tower, from which, during the Gold Rush days, a semaphore signal told of the arrival of ships through the Golden Gate.

400 square miles of San Francisco Bay
invite you to fishing, crabbing —

or yachting.

At Fisherman's Wharf you will find

king-size crabs —

king-size shells —

famous sea-food restaurants —

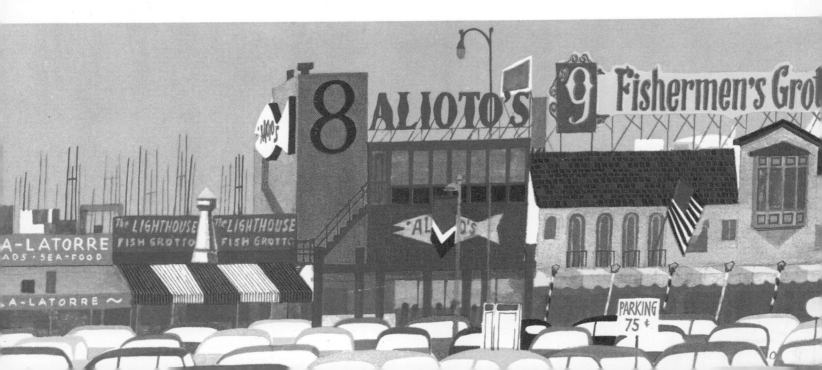

and a fleet of boats in Fisherman's Wharf.

This ship — the Balclutha — no longer sails, but is
open for boarding and viewing.

Since the ferries no longer cross the Bay, the Ferry Building now houses the World Trade Center.*

Two great bridges span San Francisco Bay:

200,000 tons of metal and 1,300,000 barrels of cement were needed to construct the San Francisco-Oakland Bay Bridge, 8 1/4 miles long.

The lower deck is for traffic into Oakland,

the upper one for traffic into San Francisco.

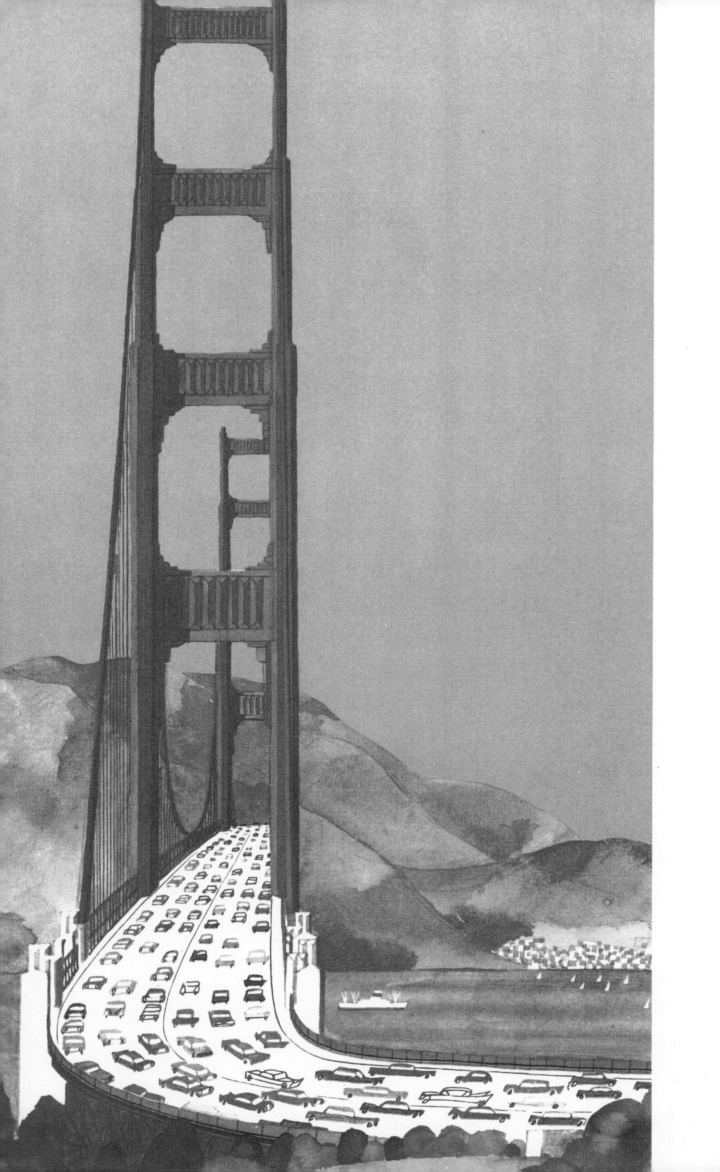

MAIN CABLE
GOLDEN GATE BRIDGE
WORLD'S LONGEST SINGLE SPAN
4,200 FT
LENGTH OF ONE CABLE 7650FT
DIAMETER 36⅜ IN
WIRES IN EACH CABLE 27,572
TOTAL WIRE USED 87,000 MI
WEIGHT OF CABLE
24,000 TONS

265 feet above the water level, crossing the
entrance of the Bay from the Pacific Ocean,
Golden Gate Bridge is the pride of the city.

The towers are as high as a 65-story building: 746 feet.

When the tide is strong, 4,500,000 cubic feet of water pour out of the Bay under the bridge every second.

The bridge is painted in a color best visible in heavy fog. This fog, which for a long time prevented the discovery of the entrance to the Bay, comes from the Pacific in the summer.

It was as late as 1775 when Captain Ayala dropped anchor where Fort Point now stands.

Presidio Terrace — a fashionable part of San Francisco

Founded in the following year, the Presidio, overlooking the Golden Gate, is the oldest settlement in the Bay area. It is now headquarters of the Sixth Army.

Also dating from 1776, Mission Dolores was established three miles inland by the Franciscan Fathers.

The ceiling was decorated by local Native Americans.

North of San Francisco the
Richmond-San Rafael Bridge
looks like a big roller coaster.

This is not a bridge, but a maze of freeways, disliked by San Franciscans
because it spoils the skyline.*

However they enjoy driving very much and so they —

DRIVE IN —

DRIVE OUT.*

This is the Japanese Tea Garden in the beautiful Golden Gate Park!

Over 1,000,000 trees grow here —

as well as some future San Francisco Giants.

Here you can see buffalo retired from the western plains —

or you can go boating on Stow Lake —

or watch sharks in Steinhart Aquarium.

The zoo, with these lovely koala bears, is not far away —

and here we are at the Pacific Ocean.

Seal Rocks made the Cliff House famous.

— but in some places you can only see it through the wires —

or perhaps through bars!

Former Federal Penitentiary — Alcatraz — known as The Rock.

San Quentin – State Prison

But the sky over San Francisco was not always blue.

On April 18, 1906, earthquake and fire
destroyed the city.

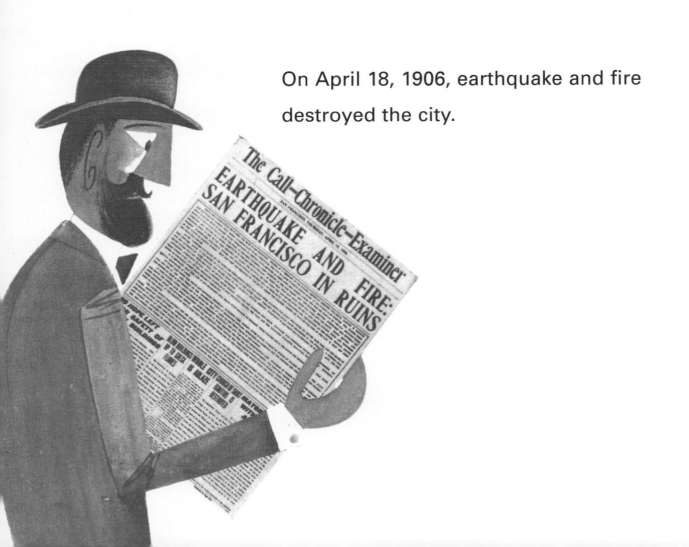

Grant Avenue with Old St. Mary's Church in ruins —

and this is how it looks today!

You enter Chinatown, the largest Chinese community outside Asia.

Grant Avenue, the paradise of window-shoppers.

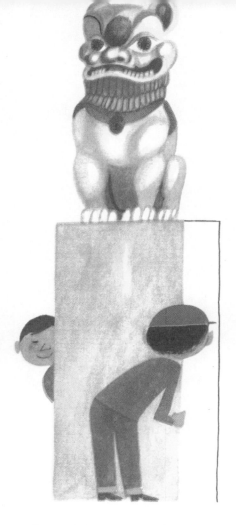

The Telephone Exchange—

the telephone booth —

old mail boxes.

Peking ducks —

fresh lau-lau from Hawaii —

and fruit from around the corner.

The heart of downtown San Francisco is Union Square with one of the
largest underground garages in the U.S.A.*

On the left of the Square — in the St.
Francis Hotel — you always receive clean
change. This machine washes it daily.

This photographer belongs to the Square —

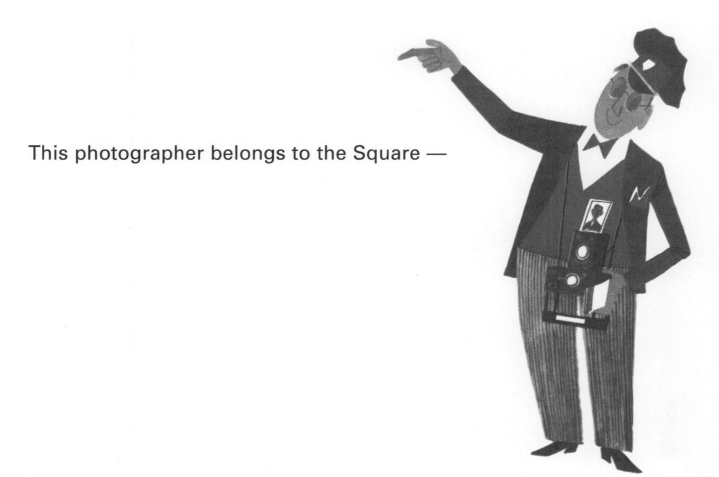

but the flowers are usually found at street corners.

The City Hall is in the Civic Center —

and the financial headquarters of the West is Montgomery Street.*

Nearly three quarters of a billion dollars in gold and silver
found their way here —

mostly aboard the Wells, Fargo & Co.
Overland stages.

Today less romantic streetcars —

and cabs —

run in downtown streets.

But from the hillsides of San Francisco have disappeared

neither gold:

California Poppy — the State flower

nor romance:

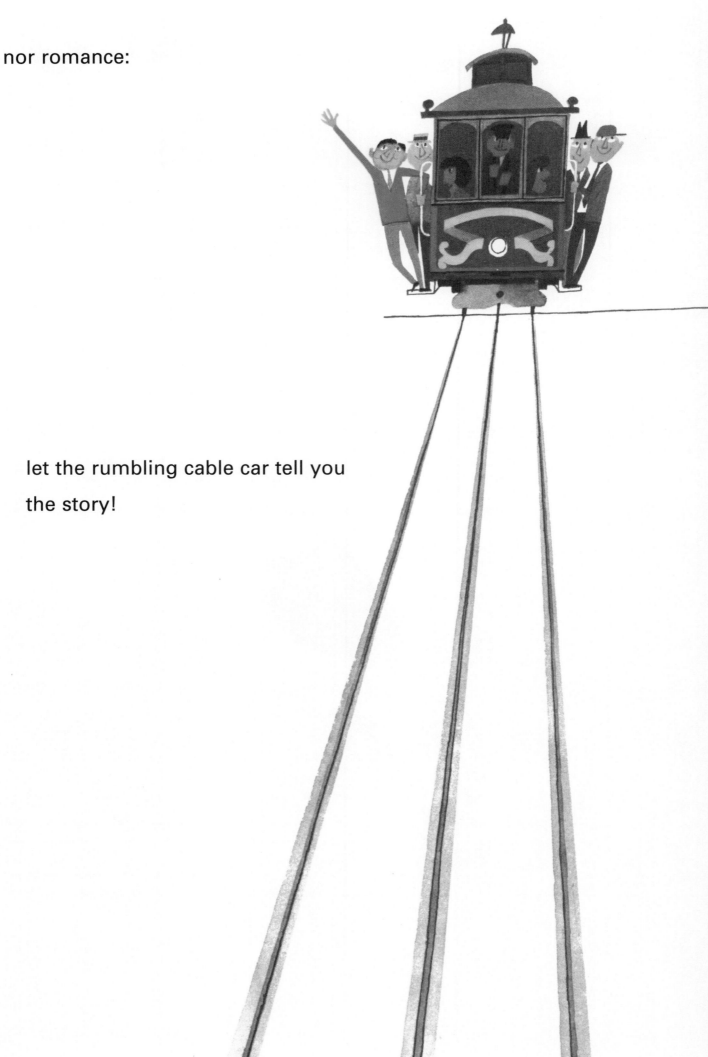

let the rumbling cable car tell you
the story!

THIS IS SAN FRANCISCO . . . TODAY!

*Page 12—Today San Francisco is the only city in the world that still operates cable cars.

*Page 23—Today the ferries cross the bay. The World Trade Center no longer exists, and the ferry building is now used as a ferry terminal and an indoor farmer's market.

*Page 34—The maze of freeways was badly damaged by the earthquake in 1989. The city voted to take it down, and today it no longer exists, nor do all the drive-ins.

*Page 54—In 1962 the Union Square Garage, the world's first underground parking facility, was the biggest of its kind in the U.S.A. Built in 1941, it was renovated in 2002.

*Page 57—Since 1972 the financial district has been home to the Transamerica Pyramid, at 600 Montgomery Street. Part of the Transamerica Center, it is a distinctive building and an international landmark.